GOD'S
IRRESISTIBLE
WORD

KENNETH HAGIN JR.

GOD'S
IRRESISTIBLE
WORD

KENNETH HAGIN JR.

Unless otherwise indicated, all Scripture quotations in this volume are from the *King James Version* of the Bible.

Third Printing 2003

ISBN 0-89276-722-7

In the U.S. write:
Kenneth Hagin Ministries
P.O. Box 50126
Tulsa, OK 74150-0126
1-888-28-FAITH
www.rhema.org

In Canada write:
Kenneth Hagin Ministries
P.O. Box 335, Station D,
Etobicoke (Toronto), Ontarioa
Canada, M9A 4X3

Contents

Preface

Never has it been more apparent than in this day and in this hour just how much the Body of Christ needs an anchor. We have that sure, fixed anchor in the Word of God! This wonderful Book, the Bible, contains God's living Word to us, His Church, and it's time we learn to trust in it with our whole hearts. I believe the day is fast approaching when God's Word will be our sole Source, for everything that can be shaken upon the earth will be shaken. But God's Word will never change! The Body of Christ needs to come to an even deeper understanding that God's Word will endure any amount of pressure we might put upon it, because it is higher than the heavens and it has been established by God Himself.

God's Word is our infallible guide! We need to renew our minds with God's irresistible Word. Then the Body of Christ will be able to go forth boldly proclaiming His Word from our lips so that we might accomplish God's purpose for us in this hour. There are so many yet who need to be saved and delivered by God's mighty power, and we have the authority to accomplish godly exploits by God's irresistible Word. Let's take our position with God's Word as our weapon and our refuge, for His Word will never fail us!

Chapter 1
God Spoke and It Stood Fast!

One of the most amazing truths in the Bible is that the world and the vast reaches of space and of the universe — all that the eye can see and *beyond* what the eye can see — were *spoken* into existence by God. The Word of God — God's own words — are absolutely irresistible! It's amazing to realize that God made everything that is — the universe, the stars, the constellations, animals, oceans, rivers — by His *Word.* He simply spoke it, and it *was;* the worlds came into being.

Nothing can stand in the way of the words that God speaks. There is no force in the universe that can refute, come against, or deny the power in God's irresistible and irrefutable Word. There is no force strong enough to nullify God's Word. The Word that God speaks is irresistible! The Bible is God's Word, and no Word of His is void of power or impossible of fulfillment!

LUKE 1:37 *(Amplified)*
37 For with God nothing is ever impossible, and no WORD from God shall be without power or impossible of fulfillment.

PSALM 33:6
6 By the WORD of the Lord were the heavens made....

PSALM 33:9
9 ... he COMMANDED, and it stood fast.

The Bible says that God's voice actually shook the mountain of Sinai when He spoke.

EXODUS 19:18
18 And mount Sinai was altogether on a smoke, because the Lord descended upon it in fire: and the smoke thereof

1

ascended as the smoke of a furnace, and the whole mount QUAKED GREATLY.

DEUTERONOMY 4:11-13
11 And ye came near and stood under the mountain; and the mountain burned with fire unto the midst of heaven, with darkness, clouds, and thick darkness.
12 And the Lord SPAKE unto you out of the midst of the fire: ye heard the VOICE OF THE WORDS, but saw no similitude; only ye heard a VOICE.
13 And he DECLARED unto you his covenant, which he commanded you to perform. . . .

Paul also records this again in Hebrews chapter 12:

HEBREWS 12:26
26 Whose VOICE then shook the earth: but now he hath promised, SAYING, Yet once more I shake not the earth only, but also heaven.

In Genesis chapter 1, we find that the very existence of the world began by God *speaking* it forth. God spoke, and whatever *He spoke* came into existence and it stood fast. Irresistible words!

GENESIS 1:3,6,7,9,11,14,15
3 And God SAID, Let there be light: AND THERE WAS LIGHT.
6 And God SAID, Let there be a firmament in the midst of the waters. . . .
7 . . . AND IT WAS SO.
9 And God SAID, Let the waters under the heaven be gathered together unto one place, and let the dry land appear: AND IT WAS SO.
11 And God SAID, Let the earth bring forth grass . . . AND IT WAS SO.
14 And God SAID, Let there be lights in the firmament

of the heaven to divide the day from the night; and let them
be for signs, and for seasons, and for days, and years:
15 And let them be for lights in the firmament of the
heaven to give light upon the earth: AND IT WAS SO.

So we see that in Genesis, the great book of beginnings, everything that was made was spoken into existence by God as He uttered *irresistible* words.

Imagine what power there is in the Word of God. God's Word cannot be opposed; it conquers and overcomes what it was sent forth by God to conquer, overcome, and defeat. God's Word is the overcomer! There is no circumstance that God's Word cannot change; there is no problem which may have tried to master you that God's Word cannot *over*master; there is no mountain or problem in your life that is too high for God's Word to surmount! The Scripture declares that even the very pillars of *heaven* tremble at the words that *God* speaks.

JOB 26:11
11 The pillars of heaven tremble and are astonished at his
REPROOF [or at His words].

Words! God used words to bring the universe into existence. How amazing! God is *GOD*. He could have created the universe any way He wanted to. But God chose *to speak* all of the worlds and the whole universe into existence. He chose to bring creation to pass by *saying* WORDS!

It is interesting to note what God *did not do* to create the universe: He didn't strike His hands together and with a resounding clap usher the worlds and the universe into existence. Or with His great creative powers and ability,

He didn't cause a tremendous crash of thunder to explode the worlds into existence in a moment. He didn't cast lightning bolts down from heaven to creatively ignite the worlds and the infinities of space into existence. No, God didn't do any of that. He just simply *spoke* WORDS: "Let there *BE.*" And when He *spoke,* the Bible says, "There *was.*"

When God says something, it happens! God spoke irresistible words that could not be refuted, that could not be denied, that could not be opposed, and what He declared, came into being. God's Word has undeniable, irrefutable, incontestable power! It can create, effect change, dismantle, and solve any problem in *your* life too!

You see, the words God speaks contain something. They contain power, strength, ability, might, and all dominion! Therefore, we need to learn to speak God's *Word!* All the needs of mankind are met, satisfied, and fully supplied in the *Word* of God.

> **PHILIPPIANS 4:19**
> 19 But my God shall supply all your need according to his riches in glory by Christ Jesus.
>
> **PHILIPPIANS 4:19** (*Amplified*)
> 19 And my God will liberally supply (fill to the full) your every need according to His riches in glory in Christ Jesus.
>
> **2 CORINTHIANS 1:20**
> 20 For all the promises of God in him are yea, and in him Amen, unto the glory of God by us.
>
> **PSALM 12:6**
> 6 The words of the Lord are pure words: as silver tried in a furnace of earth, purified seven times.

God's Word is holy. You see, words are containers.

What does a container do? A container *holds* or *contains* something. Because the Word of God is holy and pure, it contains love, joy, peace, power, ability, might — in fact, *whatever pertains to life and godliness* — God's Word contains it! *In fact,* God's Word contains within itself the power to create whatever it says it will do! No wonder God could use His words to create the universe!

However, many people don't realize that *their* words are containers too, and when they speak, they are pouring the contents of those words out all around them. The words people speak can either contain faith, happiness, joy, and peace, or they can contain hatred, unbelief, despair, and division. Words either pollute the listener, or they build up, add to, and edify those who hear them. Words people speak have an effect upon the hearers of those words.

For example, the words spoken to a child as he goes out the door to school, can help determine whether that child succeeds or fails that day. If you're constantly telling a child he's a failure and that he will never succeed in anything he does, those words will stay with him and bear fruit in his life. Kind words spoken to a husband or to a wife in the morning can either contribute to a sense of well-being or to a sense of failure; they either build up and edify, or they tear down and destroy.

A story is told of a notorious gangster who came out of the north central Texas area. When he was a boy, it was said of him that he was a mischievous child who just liked to have fun. An older gentleman who knew him as a child, commented on this gangster's life. He said, "He was not a bad boy. He was just mischievous. *People* made him what he eventually became — a gangster." He was asked,

"What do you mean, people made him into a gangster?" This older gentleman replied, "Every time something bad happened in town or something went wrong, people came looking for him because they were sure he had done it. Everyone always blamed everything bad that happened on him. They would tell him, '*You* must have done it because you're no good anyway. You're always messing up. You'll never amount to anything! When something goes wrong, you're bound to be the one who did it.' "

That young boy grew up hearing those words. Finally, one day as a young man he determined: "Every time something bad happens in this town, they come after me. So the next time the law comes after me, it'll be because I've done it!" And he began his life of crime.

If the right words had been spoken to this young man, that drive in him to be someone and to live up to people's expectations could have been channeled in a positive way to help make him a successful businessman or an asset to his community and to his country. But, instead, he died a violent death in a pool of his own blood at the end of a wasted life of crime.

How important words are!

We live in an environment of our own making — one that we have largely created by our own words. So we need to be careful to create the *right* kind of atmosphere and to speak the *right* kind of words, not only for ourselves but for the sake of our loved ones.

Have you ever been under pressure in your life and had someone speak soothing, comforting, life-giving words to you? Suddenly peace settled upon you, and all the stress and the turmoil were gone. On the other hand, you've probably also experienced feeling peaceful and tranquil and then had someone speak harsh, angry words to you and you began to feel provoked and irritated. The words you speak bear fruit. Your words determine what kind of fruit you will produce in your life and in the lives of your loved ones. *The spoken word bears fruit.*

Words create or destroy. We speak words every day and those words create an "atmosphere" around us: "I *can't.*" "It's *impossible.*" "I'll never make it." "I'm no good." "I'm so unworthy." Those words will make you a failure. But if you have the living Word of God hidden in your heart and you quote His Word, God's Word will make you a success: "I can do all things through Christ who strengthens me." "Greater is He who is in me than he who is in the world." "I have the mind of Christ" (Phil. 4:13; 1 John 4:4; 1 Cor. 2:16). God will honor His Word that you've sown in your heart, and His Word will put you over and make you a succeess in life!

The words that we speak can also leave an atmosphere charged — either in a good, healthy, positive way, or in a negative, unhealthy, and destructive way. For example, I remember an incident that occurred when I was an associate pastor at a church in Texas. My wife, Lynette, and I were responsible for home visitations. We visited one family, and we had barely stepped inside the door when we looked at one another and in an unspoken language communicated to one another, "We're intruding; we've interrupted an argument. Let's not stay too long." That house was so charged and "electrified" with the wrong spiritual atmosphere because of words spoken in anger and hostility, that we didn't want to stay there any longer than we had to!

Words are containers. It's no coincidence that God used

words to speak the worlds into existence. God in His
infinite intelligence could have chosen any method He
wanted to create the universe. But He chose *to speak* it
into existence. Words spoken by God Himself brought
forth the impossible and the miraculous; they brought
forth substance — the worlds — from nothingness.

Since words are containers, you can see how vital and
powerful it is for you to speak *God's* words, the Word of
God. Yes, the words of man contain power, but how much
more power does the Word of the living God contain?
God's Word contains *life!* Therefore, it's important for you
to be filled with God's life-giving Word — His Word of
ability and might. It's important for you to hide God's
Word in your heart.

> JOHN 6:63
> 63 It is the spirit that quickeneth; the flesh profiteth
> nothing: the WORDS that I speak unto you, they are
> SPIRIT, and they are LIFE.

> MATTHEW 24:35
> 35 Heaven and earth shall pass away, but MY WORDS
> shall not pass away.

> ISAIAH 40:8
> 8   The grass withereth, the flower fadeth: but the WORD
> of our God shall stand for ever.

> HEBREWS 4:12
> 12 For the word of God is quick, and powerful, and sharper
> than any twoedged sword, piercing even to the dividing
> asunder of soul and spirit, and of the joints and marrow,
> and is a discerner of the thoughts and intents of the heart.

Think about this for a moment: Hebrews 4:12 is saying
that the Word of God is so quick or alive and so powerful

that it can divide between the soul and the spirit of man. It's easy to distinguish the body of man from the soul or the spirit of man — that's an obvious distinction to make. But if you try to separate the *soul* from the *spirit,* you've got quite a chore ahead of you! Even trying to separate the *bones* from the *marrow* would present quite a task because these are two distinct, yet closely related elements of the body which work together almost inseparably. But *the Word of God* can separate not only joints or bones from marrow, but it can also separate the soul of man from the spirit of man! Besides that, the Bible also declares that God's Word is *quick* or alive — *full of power* in its ability to separate!

The Body of Christ has not realized the irresistible power contained in the Word of God. If Christians realized this, they would spend more time meditating and studying God's Word and giving it the first place of importance in their lives so that they could take the Word and set people free with it!

Meditating on the Word of God and speaking the irresistible Word of God is important in the plan of God. In the Book of Genesis, we saw the importance of the spoken Word of God. And the Word of God is important in the plan of God for your life too. So much more can be accomplished in your life for God's glory if you will just take care to hide God's Word in your heart. God promised that His Word would not go out and come back void, so get ready to tackle the mountains in your life and to enforce Satan's defeat upon the earth to set men and women free with this wonderful weapon God has supplied to every member of the Body of Christ!

Chapter 2
Christ Our Example

In all things, Jesus Christ is our Example. So let's look at Jesus' life to see the value He placed on speaking words anointed and inspired of God. But, first, the Bible says that Jesus *Himself* is *The Word.*

> **JOHN 1:1,14**
> 1 In the beginning was THE WORD, and THE WORD was with God, and THE WORD was God.
> 14 And THE WORD was made flesh, and dwelt among us. . . .

Also, the Bible says that Jesus Christ will come again in the clouds of glory with a shout. Very likely that means He will come with words.

> **1 THESSALONIANS 4:16**
> 16 For the Lord himself shall descend from heaven with a SHOUT. . . .

We don't know exactly what Jesus will say in that shout. He may shout, "Body of Christ, come on home," or "Let's all go!" But God is going to usher in this very important event with a shout from our Lord and Savior, Jesus Christ!

Let's see what the Bible has to say about Jesus speaking *words* — the anointed words of God. If Jesus places a high standard on the words that He spoke, then we need to be careful about the words that we speak too. We need to speak God's Word, and make sure *all* of our words are in line with God's Word — that they contain peace, love, joy, and are seasoned with **grace**.

In the New Testament, we can see that the power of
Jesus Christ and many of His miraculous works were
executed with *words*. Jesus said that He only spoke what
He heard the Father speak, and He only did what He saw
the Father do (John 5:19; John 8:28,29). Almost every
recorded miracle Jesus performed, He used words to do
it — commanding, irrefutable, irresistible *words*. Most of
the time Jesus simply commanded every hindrance or
problem to come into subjection to His Word and *whatever
it was that stood in His way* — whether it was evil spirits,
diseases, sicknesses, or the natural elements — it had to
obey Him!

At the wedding at Cana, Jesus performed His first
miracle using *words* — words that changed a natural circumstance and met a need. You remember the story: Jesus
and His disciples went to a wedding feast in Cana. When
the host needed more wine, Jesus' mother came to Him
and asked Jesus to do something about it.

JOHN 2:1-11
1   And the third day there was a marriage in Cana of
Galilee; and the mother of Jesus was there:
2   And both Jesus was called, and his disciples, to the
marriage.
3   And when they wanted wine, the mother of Jesus saith
unto him, They have no wine.
4   Jesus saith unto her, Woman, what have I to do with
thee? mine hour is not yet come.
5   His mother saith unto the servants, WHATSOEVER
HE SAITH UNTO YOU, do it.
6   And there were set there six waterpots of stone, after
the manner of the purifying of the Jews, containing two
or three firkins apiece.
7   Jesus SAITH unto them, Fill the waterpots with water.
And they filled them up to the brim.

8 And he SAITH unto them, Draw out now, and bear unto
the governor of the feast. And they bare it.
9 When the ruler of the feast had tasted the water that
was made wine, and knew not whence it was: (but the servants which drew the water knew;) the governor of the feast
called the bridegroom.
10 And saith unto him, Every man at the beginning doth
set forth good wine; and when men have well drunk, then
that which is worse; but thou hast kept the good wine until
now.
11 This beginning of miracles did Jesus in Cana of Galilee,
and manifested forth his glory; and his disciples believed
on him.

Notice that to perform this miracle, Jesus didn't call
a big prayer meeting. In fact, the Bible doesn't even record
that Jesus prayed over the wine. He didn't hold a citywide
rally, trying to get everyone to believe God to meet the
need. He didn't do anything special. The Bible records that
Jesus merely *spoke* WORDS: "Fill the waterpots. Draw
out now and drink" (vv. 7,8).

We know there was something special about the words
Jesus spoke by something His mother said: She told the
servants, "Do whatever He *tells* you" (v. 5). She was saying, "Jesus' words are special. Obey Jesus' *words.*" That's
an important point, because when Jesus spoke His
irresistible words, it was important that the hearers do
exactly what He said to do. If Jesus' instructions were
followed exactly, the results were always successful; the
miraculous came to pass, and the needs of mankind were
met. That's why Jesus' mother said, "Do whatever *He tells*
you to do." Jesus *commanded,* "Fill the pots with water."

But stop and think about it. In reality, whoever heard
of such a thing? No one had ever turned water into wine

before! If you fill a pot with *water,* you're going to get *water!* However, in simple faith and obedience, the servants drew the water and filled the pots with water. Then Jesus said, "Take the pots to the governor of the feast" (v. 8). Those servants must have placed a high value on Jesus' words in order to obey a command that in the natural didn't seem to make any sense.

How much more should *we,* the Body of Christ, value and obey Jesus' words!

Put yourself in the place of those servants: They were probably employed by the governor of the feast, or at least subject to his commands. When they ran out of wine, it was their responsibility to get more wine for the guests. So looking at this account from the servants' perspective, Jesus was asking them to do something which didn't make any sense whatsoever, at least in the natural. Jesus commanded them to take *water* to the governor of the feast, when the host had asked for *wine!*

(For our purposes, we'll not go into a discussion about what kind of wine this was; that is, whether or not it contained alcohol. We will only be concentrating on the miracle that Jesus performed, and *the way* He performed it. Be careful that you don't get caught up in needless controversy about this wine and get distracted from what really occurred here. Knowing the alcoholic content of this wine won't help you or save you; it won't bring you any real understanding of the miracle that Jesus performed here, and if you get caught up in unnecessary controversy over this point, you're likely to miss what's really important in this passage. Instead, if you'll focus on the miracle Jesus performed and get ahold of the interaction between Jesus' *words* and *obedience* to those words — *which always result in the miraculous* — that *will* bless you and cause faith to arise in your heart. The *faith* that you glean from this passage can cause a change in your heart and in your life!)

So looking at this situation just from a natural point of view, Jesus was instructing these servants to take *water* to the governor of the feast! Those servants either completely trusted Jesus' words, or else they were foolishly jeopardizing their jobs or perhaps even their lives. But the servants obeyed Jesus' *words* and did exactly as they were told to do, and that's why they reaped *supernatural* success! In fact, the wine was so good that when they gave the governor the water that had been turned into wine, he said to the bridegroom in astonishment, "Why have you saved the *best* wine for last!"

By obeying Jesus' words, the servants not only accomplished what they were commanded to do — to get more wine for the guests — but their act of obedience also won for the bridegroom the favor and the approval of the governor of the feast!

Obedience to God's Word brings the favor of God!

Words! Jesus' *irresistible* words brought about this miracle. Jesus merely *said,* "Fill the waterpots." Then He *said,* "Take it to the governor of the feast." Irresistible words were spoken — words that overcame the circumstance; words that overcame the lack and brought God's abundant provision into the situation to meet the needs of people!

God's Word can bring abundance into your life too! No matter what circumstance you face, no matter what trial seems to be plaguing you — God has the answer for you in His Word. Some of you have been struggling with the same insurmountable circumstances and obstacles for years. Oh, you've begged God for the answer, all right, but you've never really put God's Word to the test. Instead of begging God for the answer, put God's Word to work in your situation. God's Word will perform whatever it is sent forth to do! God wants to set you free so that you can go set others free!

Let's look at another miracle Jesus performed to see how He used *words* to bring about a change in an impossible situation. This was the healing of the nobleman's son in John 4:50. Notice that when Jesus healed the nobleman's son, He didn't hold a great healing service so He could effect a healing and a cure in this boy's body. He didn't fast and pray for many days. He simply looked at the nobleman and said, "Go your way. Your son will live." In fact, Jesus wasn't even in the child's presence — He just spoke words of power and the child was completely healed.

> JOHN 4:46-52
>
> 46 ... And there was a certain nobleman, whose son was sick at Capernaum.
>
> 47 When he heard that Jesus was come out of Judaea into Galilee, he went unto him, and besought him that he would come down, and heal his son: for he was at the point of death.
>
> 48 Then said Jesus unto him, Except ye see signs and wonders, ye will not believe.
>
> 49 The nobleman saith unto him, Sir, come down ere my child die.
>
> 50 Jesus SAITH unto him, Go thy way; thy son liveth. And the man believed THE WORD that Jesus had spoken unto him, and he went his way.
>
> 51 And as he was now going down, his servants met him, and told him, saying, THY SON LIVETH.

52 Then enquired he of them the hour when he began to amend. And they said unto him, Yesterday at the seventh hour the fever left him.

In Matthew chapter 14 when Jesus fed the multitude, He did it with words of faith in God's ability to supply the need, and it didn't matter how great the need was. Jesus' disciples had asked Him to send the crowds away, but Jesus told *them* to feed the people. The disciples protested that they had no provision for feeding such a large crowd. They only had five loaves of bread and two fish. How did Jesus handle the situation? He spoke faith-filled words. He prayed a blessing over the bread and the fish, broke them into fragments, and fed more than 5,000 people (Matt. 14:15-21)!

In Mark chapter 5, when Jesus raised Jairus' daughter from the dead, Jesus simply spoke to her and the child was brought back to life. He didn't ask everyone present to kneel down and pray. Prayer is good and right, but Jesus knew the power in His words, so He just spoke words of life to this child. He put everyone out of the room except the parents and the disciples who were with Him. Then Jesus simply took Jairus' daughter by the hand, and said faith-filled words: "... *Damsel, I say unto thee, arise*" (v. 41). He didn't hold a special service. He simply spoke words that were irresistible and irrefutable, and they overcame all obstacles, including death. Words! The powerful Word of God!

MARK 5:22-24,35-43
22 And, behold, there cometh one of the rulers of the synagogue, Jairus by name; and when he saw him, he fell at his [Jesus'] feet,

23 And besought him greatly, saying, My little daughter
lieth at the point of death: I pray thee, come and lay thy
hands on her, that she may be healed; and she shall live.
24 And Jesus went with him. . . .

35 . . . there came from the ruler of the synagogue's house
certain which said, Thy daughter is dead: why troublest
thou the Master any further?

36 As soon as Jesus heard the word that was spoken, he
saith unto the ruler of the synagogue, Be not afraid, only
believe.

37 And he suffered no man to follow him, save Peter, and
James, and John the brother of James.

38 And he cometh to the house of the ruler of the
synagogue, and seeth the tumult, and them that wept and
wailed greatly.

39 And when he was come in, he saith unto them, Why
make ye this ado, and weep? the damsel is not dead, but
sleepeth.

40 And they laughed him to scorn. But when he had put
them all out, he taketh the father and the mother of the
damsel, and them that were with him, and entereth in where
the damsel was lying.

41 And he took the damsel by the hand, and SAID unto
her, Talitha cumi; which is, being interpreted, Damsel, I
say unto thee, arise.

42 And straightway the damsel arose, and walked; for she
was of the age of twelve years. And they were astonished
with a great astonishment.

43 And he charged them straitly that no man should know
it; and commanded that something should be given her to
eat.

Luke chapter 5 gives the account of the man taken with
palsy who was let down through the roof on a stretcher
by four others. The house was full of people, but this man
was the only one who received his healing, even though
verse 17 says, ". . . *and the power of the Lord was present*

to heal them [all]. " Jesus didn't even lay hands on this man on the stretcher. He just *said* to him, ". . . *Man, thy sins are forgiven thee"* (v. 20).

The scribes and the Pharisees murmured against Jesus, claiming that Jesus didn't have the power to forgive sins. Jesus answered them by saying, *"Whether is easier, to say, Thy sins be forgiven thee; or to say, Rise up and walk? But that ye may know that the Son of man hath power upon earth to forgive sins, (he said unto the sick of the palsy,) I SAY unto thee, ARISE, AND TAKE UP THY COUCH, AND GO INTO THINE HOUSE"* (Luke 5:23,24).

The Bible says the man immediately got up off the couch and went into his own house glorifying God (v. 25).

In Mark 9:25, when Jesus cast the deaf and dumb spirit out of the child, He *spoke* to the spirit to come out, and it had to obey His words!

MARK 9:25-27
25 When Jesus saw that the people came running together, he REBUKED the foul spirit, SAYING unto him, Thou dumb and deaf spirit, I charge thee, come out of him, and enter no more into him.
26 And the spirit cried, and rent him sore, and CAME OUT OF HIM: and he was as one dead; insomuch that many said, He is dead.
27 But Jesus took him by the hand, and lifted him up; and he arose.

In Mark chapter 4, we read the account of Jesus and His disciples on the Sea of Galilee. Jesus and His disciples had gotten into the ship, and Jesus had given His disciples a command to cross over to the other side of the sea. A great storm arose while Jesus was asleep in the back of the ship. Jesus' disciples were terrified because of the storm. But if they had just listened to *the words* Jesus spoke to them, they wouldn't have been afraid when the storm began to rage.

> MARK 4:35-41
> 35 And the same day, when the even was come, he saith unto them, LET US PASS OVER UNTO THE OTHER SIDE.
> 36 And when they had sent away the multitude, they took him even as he was in the ship. And there were also with him other little ships.
> 37 And there arose a great storm of wind, and the waves beat into the ship, so that it was now full.
> 38 And he was in the hinder part of the ship, asleep on a pillow: and they awake him, and say unto him, Master, carest thou not that we perish?
> 39 And he arose, and rebuked the wind, and SAID unto the sea, Peace, be still. And the wind ceased, and there was a great calm.
> 40 And he said unto them, Why are ye so fearful? how is it that ye have no faith?
> 41 And they feared exceedingly, and said one to another, What manner of man is this, that even the wind and the sea OBEY HIM.

When the disciples saw that the storm was about to sink their ship, they were frightened and woke up Jesus demanding, "... *Master, careth thou not that we perish?*" (Mark 4:38). The Bible says that Jesus arose and rebuked the storm, and *it obeyed Him.* In other words, Jesus *said* something which caused a complete change in the weather. Then Jesus spoke to the sea and said, "Peace, be still." Those words were so full of the irresistible power of God that instantly there was a tremendous reaction in the skies and upon the sea, because the Bible says, "... *there was a great calm"* (v. 39).

That storm which was alarming enough to cause the disciples to fear for their lives, was calmed and subdued after Jesus spoke irresistible words full of power and commanded it to cease!

In this instance, Jesus had to rebuke His disciples for their lack of faith and trust in His Word. He said, ". . . Where is your faith — your trust, your confidence in Me, [in My veracity and My integrity]?. . ." (Luke 8:25 *Amplified*). Jesus had already spoken the instructions to pass over to the other side. Jesus was telling them, "My Word has integrity! You can count on what I say!"

In John 5:8, Jesus just spoke to the impotent man at the pool of Bethesda, saying, *". . . Rise, take up thy bed, and walk."* Jesus' compassion was reflected in His words. The Bible says, *". . . Immediately the man was made whole, and took up his bed, and walked: and on the same day was the sabbath"* (v. 9).

As we saw in the miracle Jesus performed at the marriage feast in Cana, Jesus' words had to be obeyed in order for any miracle to take place. Many times Jesus gave instructions which *had to be obeyed* before the miracle could occur. The same thing was true in order to bring about a physical healing. Sometimes Jesus effected healing by speaking words which gave direction. As Jesus' directions or instructions were obeyed, healing resulted.

For example, in the case of the blind man in John chapter 9, Jesus spoke words of instruction *which had to be obeyed* in order for that blind man to be healed.

JOHN 9:1-7
1 And as Jesus passed by, he saw a man which was blind

from his birth.
2   And his disciples asked him, saying, Master, who did
sin, this man, or his parents, that he was born blind?
3   Jesus answered, Neither hath this man sinned, nor his
parents: but that the works of God should be made
manifest in him.
4   I must work the works of him that sent me, while it is
day: the night cometh, when no man can work.
5   As long as I am in the world, I am the light of the world.
6   When he had thus SPOKEN, he spat on the ground,
and made clay of the spittle, and he anointed the eyes of
the blind man with the clay.
7   And SAID unto him, Go, wash in the pool of Siloam,
(which is by interpretation, Sent.) He went his way
therefore, and washed, and came seeing.

In this instance, Jesus spoke words of instruction to
this blind man: "... *Go, wash in the pool of Siloam ...*'
(v. 7). Jesus not only told him to go wash, but he directed
him to a specific place to wash — the pool of Siloam. He
didn't just say, "Go wash," or "Go home and wash." As
the blind man obeyed Jesus' *words* — that specific direction — the man was healed, and came again seeing!

There are many Christians today who are not receiving from God because they are not obeying the instructions given in God's Word, the Bible. They are not
following the directions and instructions God has already
laid out for them in His Word. They want to receive from
God, but at the same time they want to do things the way
they want to do them. This blind man never would have
received his healing if he had not obeyed Jesus' words and
washed in the pool of Siloam. Stop and think about it:
There may have been water right there where he and Jesus
stood talking! Or it's possible that the blind man could

have borrowed a water pot and washed in that. But, you see, none of those things would have done any good because those weren't the instructions Jesus gave him.

Many times in the Bible, Jesus spoke words giving specific direction and instruction. That's important to understand because once Jesus' words were followed exactly and acted upon, they produced miraculous results! Christians need to understand this principle, because it's obedience to the direction and instruction given in God's Word that brings salvation, healing, deliverance, peace, and success in every area of life.

If you are looking to God to do something in your life, but there's an area in His Word you have refused to obey, get in line with His Word first, and then watch God move in your behalf. It's not hard for God to perform His Word for you, but most of the time Christians have a hard time getting *in a position* to be able to receive from God!

Let's look at another passage where Jesus spoke irresistible, irrefutable words that brought comfort, health, and healing:

> LUKE 4:38,39
> 38 And he [Jesus] arose out of the synagogue, and entered into Simon's house. And Simon's wife's mother was taken with a great fever; and they besought him for her.
> 39 And he stood over her, and REBUKED the fever [that is, Jesus spoke strong, anointed *words*]; and it left her: and IMMEDIATELY she arose and ministered unto them.

Let's see what Jesus did when He was faced with the death of Lazarus. Surely in the face of His enemy, death, Jesus would do something more dramatic than just speak words!

JOHN 11:38-45

38 Jesus . . . cometh to the grave. It was a cave, and a stone lay upon it.

39 Jesus said, Take ye away the stone. Martha, the sister of him that was dead, saith unto him, Lord, by this time he stinketh: for he hath been dead four days.

40 Jesus saith unto her, Said I not unto thee, that, if thou wouldest believe, thou shouldest see the glory of God?

41 Then they took away the stone from the place where the dead was laid. And Jesus lifted up his eyes, and said, Father, I thank thee that thou hast heard me.

42 And I knew that thou hearest me always: but because of the people which stand by I said it, that they may believe that thou hast sent me.

43 And when he thus had spoken, HE CRIED WITH A LOUD VOICE, Lazarus, come forth.

44 And he that was dead came forth, bound hand and foot with graveclothes: and his face was bound about with a napkin. Jesus saith unto them, Loose him, and let him go.

45 Then many of the Jews which came to Mary, and had seen the things which Jesus did, believed on him.

Jesus prayed to the Father, and then spoke words of such miraculous quality, that Lazarus was raised from the dead.

Notice what happened when Jesus healed the lepers in Luke chapter 17.

LUKE 17:12-14

12 And as he entered into a certain village, there met him ten men that were lepers, which stood afar off:

13 And they lifted up their voices, and said, Jesus, Master, have mercy on us.

14 And when he saw them, he SAID unto them, Go shew yourselves unto the priests. And it came to pass, that, AS THEY WENT [that is, as they obeyed the word that was spoken], they were cleansed.

Jesus didn't touch the lepers; He didn't even pray for them. He didn't cause lightning to come out of heaven or cause thunder to roll. He could have done all those things. Instead, He simply spoke words of instruction, "Go show yourselves to the priest." But it was as these lepers ACTED ON HIS WORDS that they were healed. Psalm 107:20 says, *"He sent HIS WORD, and healed them, and delivered them from their destructions."* Irresistible words!

God has already sent His Word to bring you salvation, to heal you, and to overturn any situation in your life that you have been crying out to Him about. Put His Word to work in your situation!

God's Word acted upon brings results! God's Word will bring the miraculous into your life so that you can help others know that God is a God of deliverance!

Chapter 3
Whose Word Do You Trust?

Our problem is that we have learned to believe and trust in everyone else's words except *God's*. We trust people because of what they say, or we mistrust them because of what they don't say. But we usually take *people* at their word!

For example, if your employer were to call you in and tell you that you were going to get a raise amounting to $200 a week, you would be overjoyed. In fact, you'd be so excited, you'd probably run to the telephone immediately and call your wife or your husband: "Honey, my boss raised my salary $200 a week! Let's go out and buy that car we've been wanting!"

I want you to realize something. We all react like this in faith when we hear words we trust. In this instance you might not even have the money in hand yet, but because you believe the words that are spoken to you, you operate in faith on those words. Words such as these create in all of us an excitement, and because we *believe* them, we act upon them.

How much more should we believe in the Word of the Holy One who created the universe?

How many a young man playing football has heard the coach say to him, "You deserve a starting spot Friday night," and was thrilled to hear those words. He's not even in the game yet, but those words create such an excitement in him that when game time comes, he goes wild on the field.

And we've all read stories in sports about some unknown player becoming the star player overnight because someone believed in him and spoke words that filled him with confidence and tapped hidden resources of his ability. Picture this: In the middle of the game, the first-string quarterback gets hurt. The backup quarterback who's been sitting on the bench just waiting for a chance to play, finally gets to show what he can do. But he's apprehensive because he knows he's got to go in and replace the star player — the guy who's *always* the hero.

The coach calls the backup quarterback over and says to him, "I believe in you! You've got the goods! You've just never had a chance to show what you can really do. Go out there and show the people that you've got what it takes!" Words! That quarterback grabs his helmet and straps it on, and he's a running ball of fire on that field. He says to himself, *I can do it! I know I can do it! Just give me that ball!*

Words of faith and confidence from a wise coach can energize and fill a player with strength and ability he didn't even know he had! Yet we have difficulty believing THE WORD! We have difficulty acting on THE WORD! The Word of God should create more excitement in us than a coach's words of faith and encouragement create in a football player who's just been told he gets to play in the big game!

We put trust in other people's words all the time. How much more sure testimony do we have in the Word of God!

NUMBERS 23:19 (*Amplified*)
19 God is not a man, that He should tell or act a lie, neither the son of man, that He should feel repentance or compunction [for what He has promised]. Has He said, and shall He not do it? Or has He spoken and shall He not make it good?

ISAIAH 55:11
11 So shall my word be that goeth forth out of my mouth:
it shall not return unto me void, but it shall accomplish
that which I please, and it shall prosper in the thing
whereto I sent it.

God is looking for His people to have simple faith and
trust in *His Word!*

One reason many Christians don't receive from God
is that they don't take God at His Word! Or they never
really put any pressure on His Word; they try to do everything in their own strength. They have never learned just
how trustworthy the Word of God really is.

ROMANS 4:20,21 (*Amplified*)
20 No unbelief or distrust made him [Abraham] waver or
doubtingly question concerning the promise of God, but
he grew strong and was empowered by faith as he gave
praise and glory to God,
21 Fully satisfied and assured that God was able and
mighty TO KEEP HIS WORD AND TO DO WHAT HE
HAD PROMISED.

HEBREWS 10:23 (*Amplified*)
23 So let us seize and hold fast and retain without waver-
ing the hope we cherish and confess, and our acknowledg-
ment of it, for He Who promised is reliable (sure) and
FAITHFUL TO HIS WORD.

Another reason many Christians do not receive from
God is that they have never settled the question whether
or not God is *willing* to answer their petition. They may
believe He's *able*, but they are not convinced He is *willing* to answer their prayers. Some are not even sure that
the power of God is still in operation in this day! But it
is a biblical principle that before you receive, you must

believe God is willing *and* able to grant your petition. His
Word declares that He is!

> **2 CORINTHIANS 1:20**
> **20 For all the promises of God in him are yea, and in him
> Amen, unto the glory of God by us.**

Even in the natural, you must believe before you can
receive. For example, most of you probably have a bank
account. You wouldn't write a check on that account to
make a purchase unless you believed there was money in
your account, would you? On the other hand, if you
believed there was money in your account, you wouldn't
hesitate to write a check.

Your actions are based on your *beliefs.* The same thing
holds true in the supernatural realm. You believe God;
therefore, you take Him at His Word. God is faithful and
trustworthy to His Word and He can be depended upon.

We act on our faith all the time when it comes to put-
ting simple faith and trust in *other people's* words. Along
this line, I remember one time I rented a car when I was
traveling, and as I drove the car down the street, I noticed
that the gas gauge registered empty. I turned the car
around and went back to the rental agency because the
gas tank was supposed to be full when I rented it. The
people at the desk told me that there was a problem with
the fuel gauge on that particular car. When the tank was
full, the gauge still registered empty.

Based on those *words,* I drove that car out of the rental
agency. I had faith that the words those people spoke were
true. I was not driving that car based on what I could see,
because all visible evidence said the gas tank was empty.

If we can trust in and respect the words of *people,* how much more should we take *God* at His Word! Let's take God at His Word. And let's learn to act on God's Word in simple faith and obedience.

Without exception, every time Jesus' words were *believed* and *acted upon,* the results were always miraculous.

The disciples had *to learn* that they could believe and act upon Jesus' Word even in the face of every contradictory circumstance. For example, we find an account in the Bible when the disciples did take Jesus at His Word, even though what He said seemed to contradict what they believed to be true.

The disciples had been fishing all night and hadn't caught any fish, and Jesus came to them and SAID, "Let down your nets" (Luke 5:4). Peter protested because they had been fishing all night and hadn't caught any fish, so it didn't seem reasonable that they should go to all the trouble to lower their nets again. Nevertheless, Peter recognized the authority in Jesus' words, so he acted on them, even though in the natural it seemed foolish to do so. Peter honored the Master's *words.*

LUKE 5:4-9
4 Now when he [Jesus] had left speaking, he SAID unto Simon, LAUNCH OUT INTO THE DEEP, and LET DOWN YOUR NETS FOR A DRAUGHT.
5 And Simon answering said unto him, Master, we have toiled all the night, and have taken nothing: nevertheless AT THY WORD I will let down the net.
6 And WHEN THEY HAD THIS DONE, they inclosed a great multitude of fishes: and their net brake.
7 And they beckoned unto their partners, which were in the other ship, that they should come and help them. And

> **they came, and filled both the ships, so that they began
> to sink.**
> **8   When Simon Peter saw it, he fell down at Jesus' knees,
> saying, Depart from me; for I am a sinful man, O Lord.**
> **9   For he was astonished, and all that were with him, at
> the draught of the fishes which they had taken.**

When the disciples obeyed Jesus' words and His
specific directions, they caught so many fish, their nets
began to break. Not only that, but the Bible says their
ships were so full *"at the draught of fish"* that it looked
as if their ships would sink too! Jesus told the disciples
exactly where to fish, and when they followed *His* instructions, look at the results — God's miraculous abundance
and provision!

There is a biblical principle in all this for us: As we obey
the Word of the Living God, we will experience abundant
provision in our lives too!

Oh, if only God's people would put their trust in God's
infallible Word! What mighty exploits could be wrought
on this earth to set people free — to get them saved, healed,
and delivered to God's glory.

Christians, we need to get to the place in our spiritual
walk with the Lord that when we see something in His
Word or when the Word of God speaks to our hearts, we
immediately respond, "Lord, at Thy Word I will obey!"

The centurion in Matthew chapter 8 understood the
importance of Jesus' words. He not only had simple child-
like faith in Jesus, but he also had great respect and
reverence for Jesus' words. He believed those words, and
he acted on them. That's why he said, *". . . speak THE
WORD ONLY, and my servant shall be healed"* (v. 8).

MATTHEW 8:5-10

5 And when Jesus was entered into Capernaum, there came unto him a centurion, beseeching him,

6 And saying, Lord, my servant lieth at home sick of the palsy, grievously tormented.

7 And Jesus saith unto him, I will come and heal him.

8 The centurion answered and said, Lord, I am not worthy that thou shouldest come under my roof: but SPEAK THE WORD ONLY, and my servant shall be healed.

9 For I am a man under authority, having soldiers under me: and I say to this man, Go, and he goeth; and to another, Come, and he cometh; and to my servant, Do this, and he doeth it.

10 When Jesus heard it, he marvelled, and said to them that followed, Verily I say unto you, I have not found so GREAT FAITH, no, not in Israel.

This centurion had great faith in what? Jesus' words. He believed that if Jesus would only speak the Word, whatever Jesus said, *it would come to pass.* Therefore, receiving his miracle from Jesus was a settled issue with him before he ever came to Jesus. Jesus marvelled at his faith. Really, Jesus was commending the centurion because he had such simple trust in Jesus' Word, which in God's eyes is *great* faith. Jesus said, "*. . . I have not found so great faith, no, not in Israel*" (v. 10).

I believe each one of us in the Body of Christ desires to have God marvel at our faith because we have dared to take God at His Word and act upon it! That's the kind of faith that pleases God!

In every instance we have looked at in the Word of God, with *His Word* Jesus healed the sick or performed a miracle in order to meet the needs of mankind. Irresistible words!

Jesus also wrought deliverance by His Word. He cast out devils by speaking words which no devil or evil spirit could oppose.

Remember the madman of Gadara? Jesus used words to cast out the devils that possessed and held this man in bondage. Mark 5 gives the account of this madman who lived among the tombs and was constantly cutting himself and crying out. Jesus didn't go into a lengthy discourse to deliver him or call the elders of the church together for a meeting to decide what to do with the neighborhood demoniac. Jesus merely commanded the unclean spirits to come out of the man, and they departed into the swine (Mark 5:1-16).

Chapter 4
The Secret to Jesus' Irresistible Words

What gave Jesus the power to speak irresistible words? Why were His words so different from the words of any other man? We need to understand this so that we as *His Body,* His Church, can follow His example and speak God's irresistible words too. The Church of the Lord Jesus Christ needs to be speaking words which will change the course of people's lives and of nations to the glory of God. As the Body of Christ, we need to be setting people free!

What made Jesus' words irresistible? Many people think Jesus' words carried such authority and power because He is the Son of God. Although Jesus is, has always been, and will always be the Son of God, while He carried out His earthly ministry, Jesus did not do all those mighty deeds upon the earth as the Son of God. The Bible says that Jesus voluntarily laid aside His power and glory as the Son of God (Phil. 2:6-8), and ministered as a man *filled and anointed with the Holy Spirit* — the same way *we* are to minister.

The Bible says it was the anointing of the Holy Spirit that gave Jesus the miraculous quality of power and anointing upon His life and upon His ministry.

> ACTS 10:38
> 38 How God ANOINTED Jesus of Nazareth with THE HOLY GHOST and with power: who went about doing good, and healing all that were oppressed of the devil; for God was with him.

It was *the anointing* that made Jesus' words so full of power and ability and which gave His Words that

quality to be able to perform the miraculous to change
men's lives for the glory of God.

ISAIAH 10:27
27 ... the yoke shall be destroyed because of the anointing.

It's true that Jesus came to this earth to fulfill the
promises of God on behalf of mankind, but Jesus never
healed anyone until *after He was anointed by the Holy
Spirit.* He had to be anointed with the Holy Spirit in order
to minister, just as you and I must be anointed by the Holy
Spirit before we can minister.

Although Jesus, the Son of God, had a divine nature
when He walked upon the earth, He was also the Son of
man with a human nature. Jesus did not minister with His
divine attributes while He was on earth. He ministered
as *a man* anointed by the Holy Spirit. Jesus had the power
to speak irresistible words because He was filled with the
Holy Spirit. Jesus could speak irrefutable, incontestable
words full of power to set mankind free because of the
anointing. He spoke *anointed* words — words that were
filled with the Spirit of God. They were God's words!

Let's retrace for a moment how Jesus received the
anointing of the Holy Spirit. Jesus became anointed at the
Jordan River when the Holy Spirit in the form of a dove
descended upon Him (Matt. 3:16). This was when Jesus
received the *anointing* to minister. In the Old Testament
when a person was to be anointed to perform a certain task
or to stand in a certain office, oil was poured upon him,
representing the anointing of the Spirit of God. For example, Samuel went down to Jesse's house to anoint David
as king. Samuel poured oil upon David, anointing him to

be king over Israel (1 Sam. 16:1-13).

I remember reading a story about a man who had read in the Bible that it was scriptural to anoint the sick with oil. He knew someone who was sick, so he got a big quart-sized bottle of olive oil, went to the sick man's house, and poured that whole bottle of oil on top of the sick man's head! The man was totally healed — although it wasn't the oil that healed the man — it was *faith* that healed him. God says it's *faith* that pleases Him (Heb. 11:6). (The man got healed, but I don't know how good that oil was for his clothes!)

Throughout the Old Testament, you'll find that men were anointed with oil in order to stand in certain offices, to fulfill sacred functions, or to perform sacred tasks.

In Matthew chapter 3 when Jesus was anointed with the Holy Spirit, God spoke from heaven confirming that He had anointed His Son Jesus: *". . . This is my beloved Son, in whom I am well pleased"* (v. 17).

Immediately after that, Jesus was directed by the Holy Spirit into the wilderness. In Luke chapter 4, we are given the account of Jesus' temptation by the devil in the wilderness. It is important for us to look at this passage in our study of words because of the way Jesus dealt with the devil — by anointed words!

But just as a side thought, notice that Jesus had been fasting for forty days, and Satan was right there to tempt Him. As a practical word of caution — many times it's during those times of fasting and waiting on God when you need to exercise some wisdom. Many times that's when people are most likely to be deceived and to see images or hear voices that are not of God, especially if they are not rooted and grounded in the Word. So as a word of caution when you're fasting — make sure what you see and hear is from God and not from the enemy. You do that by being rooted and grounded in God's Word, and by making sure your spiritual experiences line up with the Word of God!

Jesus, of course, recognized that it was the devil tempting him, and rebuked Satan. But notice that Jesus overcame the temptations of the devil with the Word of God. Jesus answered Satan's temptation with the words: *"Get thee behind me Satan, FOR IT IS WRITTEN..."* (Luke 4:1-13). Jesus combated the devil with the Word of God.

That should be a lesson to every one of us too. In dealing with Satan, we are to use God's Word. Satan cannot oppose God's Word because it has been forever established.

> **PSALM 119:89**
> 89 FOR EVER, O Lord, thy Word is settled in heaven.

God's Word is irresistible. It will accomplish whatever it is sent to accomplish — including defeating the enemy in any test, temptation, or circumstance you may be facing in your life. God's Word is matchless!

The anointed Word of God will bring the results and solve the problems in your life which have perplexed you for so long, if only you will dare to believe God!

> **ISAIAH 55:11**
> 11 So shall my WORD be that goeth forth out of my mouth: IT SHALL NOT return unto me void, but IT SHALL ACCOMPLISH that which I please, and it shall prosper in the thing whereto I sent it.

> **ISAIAH 55:11** *(Amplified)*
> 11 So shall My word be that goes forth out of My mouth;

it shall not return to Me void — without producing any effect, useless — but it shall accomplish that which I please and purpose, and it shall prosper in the thing for which I sent it.

Jesus walked away from the devil's temptation triumphant, defeating Satan with God's Word, and then Jesus returned in the power of the Spirit to Galilee.

The power of the Spirit is where the anointing is! If you live with the Holy Spirit fully in charge in your life, you will *abide* in the anointing of God. If you are abiding in the Spirit, you will move in the Spirit and minister to the needs of people with the anointing of the Holy Spirit!

The power of the Spirit dominated Jesus' life because He lived and walked in the Spirit. Jesus practiced abiding in the Spirit. The result of a lifestyle dominated by the Spirit of God is found in Acts 10:38: "*... God anointed Jesus ... with power: who went about DOING GOOD, and HEALING all that were oppressed of the devil....*" Because of that, "*... there went out a fame of him through all the region round about*" (Luke 4:14).

When Jesus came to His hometown of Nazareth, as was His custom, He taught in the synagogue. In this passage in Luke, Jesus is reading from the Book of the prophet Isaiah (Isa. 61:1).

LUKE 4:18-22
18 The Spirit of the Lord is upon me, because he hath anointed me to preach the gospel to the poor; he hath sent me to heal the brokenhearted, to preach deliverance to the captives, and recovering of sight to the blind, to set at liberty them that are bruised,
19 To preach the acceptable year of the Lord.
20 And he closed the book, and he gave it again to the

minister, and sat down. And the eyes of all them that were
in the synagogue were fastened on him.
21 And he began to SAY unto them, This day is this
scripture fulfilled in your ears.
22 And all bare him witness, and wondered at the gracious
words which proceeded out of his mouth. . . .

It is significant that when Jesus returned to His hometown, the first thing He did was to proclaim who He is.
And the words Jesus used to introduce Himself in His
hometown were God's Word: *"The Spirit of the Lord is
upon me, because he hath ANOINTED me . . ."* (Luke
4:18). Jesus began His public ministry using God's powerful Word declaring that He was anointed by the Holy
Spirit of God.

Then Jesus declared what the Holy Spirit had anointed
Him to do: To preach, to teach, and to bring deliverance
to the captives. Jesus set in motion what His aim and His
purpose on this earth were — with captivating, anointed
words — because the Bible says that all the eyes of those
in the synagogue were fastened upon Him. After hearing
the proclamation, *"This day is this scripture fulfilled in
your ears"* (v. 21), not one sick person should have left that
place without receiving healing! In fact, the minute Jesus
uttered those words, revival should have broken out in that
place!

In Mark 6:5,6 we are told why there was no revival.
It says, *"And he [Jesus] could there do no mighty work,
save that he laid his hands upon a few sick folk, and healed
them. And he marvelled because of their UNBELIEF. And
he went round about the villages, teaching."*

Every time Jesus' words were *believed* and *acted upon,*
the results were miraculous. But these people were in

doubt and unbelief. They didn't take Jesus at His word, so they couldn't receive what God had already freely provided for them. So in order to dispel the doubt and unbelief in the people, Jesus had to teach the Word of God in the villages and in the towns. Jesus knew that the only way to deal with doubt and unbelief was with God's quick, powerful, and irresistible Word!

If we think about Jesus' life for a moment, we can also understand how Jesus *maintained* the anointing that was on His life. Many times in the Word of God, we read that Jesus would frequently steal away to spend private time in prayer with the Father. Jesus was constantly abiding in the Father's Presence in order to maintain the anointing upon His own life and ministry. Let's look at some of those instances:

> **MATTHEW 14:23**
> 23 And when he had sent the multitudes away, he went up into a mountain apart to pray: and when the evening was come, he was there alone.
>
> **LUKE 6:12**
> 12 And it came to pass in those days, that he [Jesus] went out into a mountain to pray, and continued all night in prayer to God.
>
> **MATTHEW 26:36**
> 36 Then cometh Jesus with them unto a place called Gethsemane, and saith unto the disciples, Sit ye here, while I go and pray yonder.

We've seen the value Jesus placed on words because, first, He *is* the Word. Second, we've seen Jesus using Holy Spirit anointed words to undo the works of the enemy to set men and women free. But now let's look at a scripture which tells us specifically the value that Jesus placed on words — words which line up with the Word of God and words that are anointed by the Holy Spirit and full of power. In this scripture, Jesus is not only telling us the value *He* places on words, He is also giving us direction and instruction about the words *we* speak.

> MARK 11:22-24
> 22 ... Have faith in God.
> 23 For verily I say unto you, That whosoever shall SAY unto this mountain, Be thou removed, and be thou cast into the sea; and shall not doubt in his heart, but shall believe that those things which he SAITH shall come to pass; he shall have whatsoever he SAITH.
> 24 Therefore I say unto you, What things soever ye desire when ye pray, believe that ye receive them, and ye shall have them.

For the moment, let's not look at the part of this scripture which deals with *believing* with the heart. That's important, but for the purpose of our study, let's see what Jesus has to say about *saying* or *speaking.*

In this scripture, Jesus is telling *us* — the Body of Christ — to speak words. He is telling us that *power* and *faith* are released through our words, and He is telling us that faith — the God-kind of faith — speaks out what it believes according to and in line with the Word of God.

We see this same account in Matthew chapter 21.

> MATTHEW 21:18-22
> 18 Now in the morning as he returned into the city, he hungered.
> 19 And when he saw a fig tree in the way, he came to it, and found nothing thereon, but leaves only, and SAID unto it, Let no fruit grow on thee henceforward for ever. And

presently the fig tree withered away.

20 And when the disciples saw it, they marvelled, saying, How soon is the fig tree withered away!

21 Jesus answered and said unto them, Verily I say unto you, If ye have faith, and doubt not, ye shall not only do this which is done to the fig tree, but also if ye shall SAY unto this mountain, Be thou removed, and be thou cast into the sea; it shall be done.

22 And all things, whatsoever ye shall ask in prayer, believing, ye shall receive.

Jesus spoke anointed words to that fig tree — words that were in line with the will of God — and that fig tree had to obey Him.

Speaking God's irresistible Word brings results. That doesn't mean we are to go out and start cursing trees that aren't bearing fruit and demanding that they wither and die! The key here is that Jesus spoke under the inspiration of the Holy Spirit and He spoke in line with God's will in every situation. It's the *principle* that we need to be aware of: God's Word has power! We, as the Body of Christ, are to speak anointed words of power to set the captives free!

Chapter 5
Changed From Mere Men
To Men of Power!

God *is,* has always been, and always *will be.* His power is infinite, and His Word is full of power that cannot be refuted or denied. There are many scriptures which show that the anointed Word of God goes forth and changes things. The Bible is *the irresistible Word of God.*

As we have seen, this is evident from the Book of Genesis where the Bible records that God spoke the worlds into existence with His Word, to the New Testament where it is recorded that God anointed His Son, Jesus Christ of Nazareth, to speak irresistible words to set men and women free. Jesus spoke God's words and brought healing and deliverance and changed men's lives. In fact, because He *is* the Word, Jesus changed the course of history!

Jesus, in turn, gave the same power and authority to speak irresistible words — God's Word — to His disciples. Throughout the Bible God uses words and anoints people to speak words to achieve His purposes for His glory. And we will see in the Acts of the Apostles that when the Apostles spoke God's Word, the Word brought about dramatic changes to God's glory.

But before the disciples could speak God's Word with power and authority, they had to receive the same Holy Spirit that Jesus received. Before Jesus ascended into heaven, He promised His disciples that the Holy Spirit with His anointing power would come upon them and abide with them: *"And I will pray the Father, and he shall give you another Comforter, that he may abide with you*

45

for ever" (John 14:16).

Jesus also declared to His disciples what the anointing on their lives would accomplish for God's glory:

> **JOHN 14:12**
> 12 Verily, verily, I say unto you, He that believeth on me, the works that I do shall he do also; and greater works than these shall he do; because I go unto my Father.

The disciples became anointed with power from on High as they obeyed Jesus' instructions and tarried at Jerusalem to be filled with the Holy Spirit.

> **ACTS 1:4,5**
> 4   And, [Jesus] being assembled together with them, commanded them that they should not depart from Jerusalem, but wait for the promise of the Father, which, saith he, ye have heard of me.
> 5   For John truly baptized with water; but ye shall be baptized with the Holy Ghost not many days hence.

As the disciples obeyed Jesus' words, the Holy Spirit was poured out upon them. And as soon as the disciples received the anointing power of the Holy Spirit upon their lives, they were dramatically changed! No longer were they mere fishermen and public officials. With the anointing of the Holy Spirit they became transformed into holy men of power. We see throughout the Acts of the Apostles that the disciples healed the sick, brought deliverance to the captives, and changed nations as they proclaimed the gospel of the Lord Jesus Christ.

How did the disciples maintain the anointing of the Holy Spirit upon their lives? The answer is found in Acts chapter 6. You'll find as you read the Book of Acts, that the disciples gave themselves continually to prayer and to the study of the Word in order to *maintain* that anointing. The disciples' prayer life and their dedication to the Word of God was the key to the anointing and power of God in their lives.

ACTS 6:4
4 But we will give ourselves continually to PRAYER, and to the ministry of THE WORD.

It's no coincidence that with that kind of lifestyle, the disciples walked in the anointing of God. When they spoke God's irresistible Word, people were healed and delivered. *The Word of God spoken with the anointing of God is full of power.*

Now let's look at some of the irresistible words the disciples spoke and the supernatural acts they wrought because they were anointed from on High with the Holy Spirit.

Early in the Book of Acts, we read that Peter and John came to the temple to pray as was their habit. There was a lame man who was sitting at the Gate called Beautiful:

ACTS 3:1-10
1 Now Peter and John went up together into the temple at the hour of prayer, being the ninth hour.
2 And a certain man lame from his mother's womb was carried, whom they laid daily at the gate of the temple which is called Beautiful, to ask alms of them that entered into the temple;
3 Who seeing Peter and John about to go into the temple asked an alms.
4 And Peter, fastening his eyes upon him with John, said, Look on us.
5 And he gave heed unto them, expecting to receive

something of them.

6   Then Peter said, Silver and gold have I none; but such
as I have give I thee: In the name of Jesus Christ of
Nazareth rise up and walk.

7   And he took him by the right hand, and lifted him up:
and immediately his feet and ankle bones received strength.

8   And he leaping up stood, and walked, and entered with
them into the temple, walking, and leaping, and praising
God.

9   And all the people saw him walking and praising God;

10   And they knew that it was he which sat for alms at the
Beautiful gate of the temple: and they were filled with
wonder and amazement at that which had happened unto
him.

When Peter came upon this lame man, he simply said
to him, "... *Silver and gold have I none; but such as I have
give I thee: In the name of Jesus Christ of Nazareth rise
up and walk*" (v. 6). And the Bible says that immediately
the lame man's feet and ankle bones were strengthened,
and he rose up walking and leaping and praising God
(vv. 7,8).

Peter didn't pray over the lame man; Peter had already
prayed. His was a lifestyle of prayer. We saw in Acts 6:4
that the disciples gave themselves continually to prayer
and to the ministry of the Word. Because of Peter's prayer
life and his dedication to the Word of God, he was already
charged with power by the Holy Ghost! So at the Gate
called Beautiful, Peter merely spoke irresistible words full
of power, and the anointing of God made that lame man
completely whole!

This incident is recorded in Acts chapter 3. In Acts
chapter 6, we read that the Church had grown so much
that the many added administrative duties were becoming

burdensome to the disciples. Instead of allowing these responsibilities to jeopardize their study of the Word and their lives of prayer which could affect the anointing on their lives to teach and to preach, the disciples chose seven men of good report who had the anointing of God on their lives to carry out these practical duties.

> ACTS 6:2-4
> 2   Then the twelve called the multitude of the disciples unto them, and said, It is not reason that we should leave the word of God, and serve tables.
> 3   Wherefore, brethren, look ye out among you seven men of honest report, full of the Holy Ghost and wisdom, whom we may appoint over this business.
> 4   But we will give ourselves continually to prayer, and to the ministry of the word.

The disciples had learned the lesson well from Jesus that the anointing on their lives had to be maintained by close fellowship and communion with God in prayer and in the Word. That's why we see the disciples used so mightily in the Acts of the Apostles. Their words were powerful and mighty because they spent time communing with God.

Let's look at another instance where we see the anointing on one of the disciples' lives. Peter moved in the might and power of the Holy Spirit when Dorcas died. Peter prayed and then spoke God's Word in authority with the anointing of the Holy Spirit upon him, and Dorcas was raised from the dead.

> ACTS 9:36-42
> 36 Now there was at Joppa a certain disciple named Tabitha, which by interpretation is called Dorcas: this

woman was full of good works and almsdeeds which she
did.
37 And it came to pass in those days, that she was sick,
and died: whom when they had washed, they laid her in an
upper chamber.
38 And forasmuch as Lydda was nigh to Joppa, and the
disciples had heard that Peter was there, they sent unto
him two men, desiring him that he would not delay to come
to them.
39 Then Peter arose and went with them. When he was
come, they brought him into the upper chamber: and all
the widows stood by him weeping, and shewing the coats
and garments which Dorcas made, while she was with them.
40 But Peter put them all forth, and kneeled down, and
prayed; and turning him to the body SAID, Tabitha,
ARISE. And she opened her eyes: and when she saw Peter,
she sat up.
41 And he gave her his hand, and lifted her up, and when
he had called the saints and widows, presented her alive.
42 And it was known throughout all Joppa; and many
believed in the Lord.

We also see the anointing on Paul's words as he
traveled on his missionary journeys. Paul simply spoke
invincible words of power and authority and circumstances, situations, and men's lives were changed.

For example, in Philippi a maiden who was possessed
with a spirit of divination followed the disciples, crying
out, "... *These men are the servants of the most high God,
which shew unto us the way of salvation*" (Acts 16:17).
Paul was vexed in his spirit that the devil was advertising
for him, and he finally turned around to the woman and
addressed the evil spirit, "... *I command thee in the name
of Jesus Christ to come out of her* ..." (Acts 16:18). And
the Bible says, "... *he came out the same hour*" (v. 18).

Words! Because Paul walked so closely with God, He merely spoke words full of power to this evil spirit using that Name which is above every name — the Name of Jesus!

As long as the disciples were full of the Holy Spirit and that anointing was burning brightly in their lives, they spoke forth *God's Word,* and those words were irresistible and irrefutable. But, remember, the words spoken from the disciples' lips produced dramatic results to God's glory because they were spoken in line with God's Word and His will. Their words were spoken to set men free from the oppression of the enemy, not for personal gain or to exalt themselves.

> ACTS 14:8-10
> 8   And there sat a certain man at Lystra, impotent in his feet, being a cripple from his mother's womb, who never had walked:
> 9   The same heard Paul speak: who stedfastly beholding him, and perceiving that he had faith to be healed,
> 10 Said with a loud voice, Stand upright on thy feet. And he leaped and walked.

Because this man had the faith to be healed, Paul could speak to him words of power and anointing, and the Bible says, the man leaped and walked and was made perfectly whole.

The disciples spoke God's powerful, irresistible Word under the anointing *of the Holy Spirit.* No man is to take credit for the mighty works that God brings to pass through His Word! It's the anointing of the Holy Spirit that breaks the yoke!

Chapter 6
Power and Authority
Belong to the Church

At His ascension, Jesus gave the same power and authority to speak God's irresistible Word to the Church — the whole Body of Believers. Just before Jesus ascended to the right hand of the Father, He said, "... *He that believeth on me, the works that I do shall he do also; and greater works than these shall he do; because I go unto my Father*" (John 14:12).

Also, we know that this same power and authority has been given to the Church because Jesus declared it with words:

> **MARK 16:17,18**
> 17 And these signs shall follow them that believe; In my name shall they cast out devils; they shall speak with new tongues;
> 18 They shall take up serpents; and if they drink any deadly thing, it shall not hurt them; they shall lay hands on the sick, and they shall recover.

One of the greatest messages the Church needs to hear in this hour is that through the Lord Jesus Christ we possess the power to speak the irresistible Word of God with power and authority. Why did God give the Church this authority? So we could heap up riches and power for ourselves? NO! So we could set this world on fire with the news that Jesus Christ has come to seek and to save that which was lost, and to set men and women free from the power of the enemy. Satan has to bow his knee to the Name of Jesus! (Phil 2:9-11).

The Word of God spoken through the lips of the members of the Body of Christ will set in motion mighty wonders upon this earth for the benefit of mankind!

Many in the Body of Christ are not aware of the authority they really possess because of the Word of God, and they are not taking what is rightfully theirs — that which was legally bought and paid for at the Cross of Calvary. They are still trying "to believe" for what already belongs to them, when all they really need to do is to take God at His Word and speak the Word forth in the anointing of the Holy Spirit! The Word will accomplish what it has been sent forth to accomplish! Then they need to take that same authority and go set the captives free — those who are enslaved to Satan and who have never heard the good news of the gospel.

The Body of Christ has the authority to speak God's Word in power because we are anointed with the Holy Spirit, and it's the anointing that breaks the yoke of bondage. As we walk after the Spirit and not after the flesh, consecrating and dedicating ourselves to lives of holiness — God's Word spoken from our lips will have power!

And we must remember that when Jesus gave power and authority to the Church, He didn't give that power to just one local body, or just to *certain* members of the Body of Christ! No, He gave authority and power to His Body — the Church, the Ekklesia — the called out ones. Those who are born again, blood-bought, and blood-washed have the authority to declare God's Word in boldness so that we might have life and have it more abundantly, and bring the good news of that life to others!

Many of you have learned the secret of speaking God's irresistible Word. But every Christian ought to realize the importance of God's Word in their lives. Every Christian has the blood-bought right to speak God's irrefutable Word with boldness. Get ahold of that important truth: Every member of the Body of Christ can speak words that are anointed; words that bring forth miraculous results of life and liberty; words which release others from bondage; and words that accomplish whatever they are sent to do — *as long as they are based on God's Word.*

If you base your words on the promises in God's Word, and you speak them with the anointing of the Holy Spirit, you will get results! The Bible promises us this.

Let's look at the anointing which is promised to every believer.

JOHN 16:13
13 Howbeit when he, THE SPIRIT OF TRUTH, is come, he will guide you into all TRUTH: for he shall not speak of himself; but whatsoever he shall hear, that shall he speak: and he will shew you things to come.

1 JOHN 2:27
27 But the ANOINTING which ye have received of him abideth in you . . . the same ANOINTING teacheth you of all things, and is truth, and is no lie, and even as it hath taught you, ye shall abide in him.

1 JOHN 2:20
20 But ye have an UNCTION [anointing] from the Holy One, and ye know all things.

2 CORINTHIANS 1:21
21 Now he which stablisheth us with you in Christ, and hath ANOINTED us, is God.

God's Word spoken with the anointing of the Holy Spirit will be irresistible to the men and women of this world whose eyes have been blinded to the glorious light of the gospel. God's Word is quick and powerful and sharper than any twoedged sword! Of course, we realize that God has given people free will and the right to choose their own destiny — whether they will spend eternity with Him or in hell. God will never violate man's free choice. But God will provide mankind with every opportunity to choose Him and to choose eternal life!

Many people have heard teachings about the power of words and particularly about the power contained in God's Word, and they've said, "Oh, *if only* that were true!" I'm talking about born-again, Spirit-filled people! And then they begin to magnify the devil by always talking about what he is doing in their lives, instead of what God is doing. Many times I hear people giving the enemy such credit by telling all the horrible things he is trying to bring to pass in their lives, when they should be acknowledging God and giving Him praise and glory for all that He has done for them. We should be concentrating on what God is doing instead of on what the devil is doing!

Begin to recognize God at work in your life! Magnify what God is doing instead of focusing on what the devil is trying to do. Begin declaring, "Greater is He that is in me than he that is in the world." "I am an overcomer in Christ Jesus." Speak out boldly in the face of adverse circumstances, "I am more than a conqueror in Christ Jesus." "God always gives me the victory in Christ Jesus" (Rom. 8:37; 2 Cor. 2:14). Begin to speak the irresistible Word of God! It will make you an overcomer in life.

And if Satan tries to taunt you with past mistakes you've already asked God's forgiveness for — quote God's Word to him. Let God's Word fight your battles for you! God's Word is the sword of the Spirit!

1 JOHN 1:9
9 If we confess our sins, he is faithful and just to forgive us our sins, and to cleanse us from all unrighteousness.

PSALM 103:12
12 As far as the east is from the west, so far hath he removed our transgressions from us.

If God has removed your sins as far as the east is from the west, that means He has removed them *entirely* because the east and the west never meet! Your sins can't be found if they've been remitted!

Chapter 7
Maintain the Anointing

We've seen how Jesus our Example maintained the anointing upon His life, so that His Words were full of power. We've also seen how the disciples set themselves aside to seek God to keep the fire of the Holy Spirit aflame in their lives. Now we need to look at some practical ways that we, the Body of Christ, can maintain the anointing so our words do not lose their effectiveness and we can accomplish God's purposes for our lives upon this earth.

We have already seen from the Scriptures that sometimes Jesus gave instructions, and *as those instructions were carried out,* the results were miraculous. Whatever the need, it was granted as the individual or individuals obeyed Jesus' words and followed His specific *instructions.* Therefore, we can see that in order to speak the irresistible words of God and to maintain the anointing upon our lives, the Body of Christ will have to obey the instructions that have been given to us in the Word of God.

However, before a person can enter into the anointing of God, he must be born again. You will never be able to speak God's irresistible Word with power and authority unless you've been born again by the blood of the Lord Jesus Christ. If you've never been born again, you're not even in the "game" yet, so to speak; you're still sitting on the sidelines just watching the touchdowns. You can't score any goals if you're sitting on the bench! You can't win any gold medals or win any races if you're sitting on the sidelines. The people who achieve victory and win are those who get in the game!

So in order to win in life, you must be born again into

God's family. You've got to become a part of His team.
You can't win if you're not a part of the team.

Also, you need to be baptized in the Holy Spirit. That's
where the real anointing power comes from. Just as Jesus
and the disciples received the Holy Spirit to anoint them
to minister, so also must we be anointed by the Holy Spirit.

And then, the Bible says we are to stay filled with the
Spirit by continually recharging ourselves by praying in
the Spirit and building ourselves up on our most holy faith.
That keeps the anointing flowing every day.

JUDE 20
**20 But ye, beloved, building up yourselves on your most
holy faith, praying in the Holy Ghost.**

Many Christians neglect to keep in close enough com-
munication and fellowship with God; consequently, their
prayers become ineffective and their words just seem to
bounce off the ceiling and go nowhere. Yes, the anointing
of the Spirit of God rests upon the life of the Christian,
because Jesus promised us He would never leave us or for-
sake us (Heb. 13:5). But in order to be used mightily of
God, we must also *keep* the anointing of God aglow in our
lives. We do that by meditating on the Word and by living a life of prayer and consecration to God.

In the Bible, the Word of God has been referred to as
fire. The Holy Spirit and the anointing of God are also
sometimes referred to as "fire."

JEREMIAH 23:29 (*Amplified*)
**29 Is not MY WORD like FIRE [that consumes all that
cannot endure the test]? says the Lord, and like a hammer
that breaks in pieces the rock [of most stubborn resistance]?**

LUKE 3:16

16 John answered, saying unto them all, I indeed baptize you with water; but one mightier than I cometh, the latchet of whose shoes I am not worthy to unloose: he shall baptize you with THE HOLY GHOST and with FIRE.

Therefore, if you want to speak irresistible words and see mighty things come to pass in your life and in the lives of others to the glory of God, you've got to keep the fire of the Holy Spirit burning strongly in your life.

Keeping the anointing burning brightly in your life is like keeping a fire going strong. A fire can die down until it's just a bed of faintly glowing embers. When a fire dies down, you have to get close to it before you can feel any warmth coming from it at all. If the fire is allowed to get too low, you won't even be able to see or feel any evidence of a fire at all. Eventually, it will go out if no one puts fuel on it. However, if you put kindling wood on a bed of glowing embers, you will soon have a roaring fire. Then, I guarantee, you'll feel the warmth from that fire!

The same thing can happen with the anointing of the Holy Spirit on our lives. The anointing "fire" of the Holy Spirit can die down like a bed of embers that has never been fueled, until we lose *the sense* of the anointing on our lives. The Holy Spirit doesn't leave us, but that anointing just isn't as strong as it was. When we allow the fire of the Holy Spirit to wane in our lives, it means we've probably neglected to fuel that "fire" with continual prayer and meditation in the Word. The result is that the anointing is not so evident upon our lives or upon our words when we speak.

When the anointing of God is no longer on your words,

you can speak all day long, and nothing will happen. Begin to fuel that fire of the Holy Spirit with prayer and meditation in God's Word, and watch the flame begin to grow and consume you once again in holy fervor! Then when you speak God's Word, things will begin to happen in your life! It all depends on how much you fuel that holy "fire" on the inside of you so it can *grow* and *glow* to the glory of God.

Also, in order to maintain the anointing you will have to renew your mind with the Word of God. God's Word must become a part of your everyday life — a part of your *lifestyle.* I'm not talking about occasionally grabbing a proverb or a scripture out of a "promise" box. I'm not talking about occasionally quoting a few "faith confessions" either. Those are both good things to do, but they're not enough. I'm talking about reading, meditating, and studying God's Word every day.

> **2 TIMOTHY 2:15**
> 15 Study to shew thyself approved unto God, a workman that needeth not to be ashamed, rightly dividing the word of truth.

> **JOSHUA 1:8**
> 8 This book of the law shall not depart out of thy mouth; but thou shalt meditate therein day and night, that thou mayest observe to do according to all that is written therein; for THEN thou shalt make thy way prosperous, and THEN thou shalt have good success.

> **PSALM 1:1-3**
> 1 Blessed is the man that walketh not in the counsel of the ungodly, nor standeth in the way of sinners, nor sitteth in the seat of the scornful.
> 2 But his delight is in the law of the Lord; and in his law doth he meditate DAY and NIGHT.

> 3 And he shall be like a tree planted by the rivers of water, that bringeth forth his fruit in his season; his leaf also shall not wither; and WHATSOEVER HE DOETH SHALL PROSPER.

Along with my other studying, I have certain scriptures that I read every day because they help me maintain a walk in the Spirit. And the first thing I do when I get to my office in the morning is to shut the door and read these scriptures and have fellowship with my heavenly Father.

Unless you make time in your day for the Word of God, you will not be able to maintain a lifestyle of walking in the Spirit. You can be so taken up in the cares of the ministry or in a life of well-doing, that the anointing on your life can wane. But if you are faithful to read God's Word and to meditate on it, the Word will get down into your heart. That's when God's Word becomes life-giving *to you.* And that's when God's Word becomes effective in your life because Jesus said, *"If ye abide in me, and MY WORDS abide in you, ye shall ask what ye will, and it shall be done unto you"* (John 15:7). So before you can speak God's Word, you must know what God's Word says, and it must be *abiding* in you.

How do you get to know God's Word? How do you learn it? How does God's Word become a part of you and a part of your lifestyle? By continually taking time to hide it in your heart! That doesn't necessarily mean that you must set out *to memorize* the entire Bible, although memorizing the Word is good. But it means that as you renew your mind and edify your spirit with the Word of God, the Word becomes so much a part of you that when you face a crisis in life, the Word automatically comes out of you! We know this is true because the Bible says that what you have in your heart will eventually come out your mouth (Matt. 12:34).

So get filled up with God's Word! Then in the crises and tests and trials of life, God's Word will be your anchor enabling you to remain stable under any pressure that may come. You will become as unmovable as God's Word is! God's Word has never moved!

Does God's Word abide in *your* heart? Does the anointing power of the Holy Spirit rest strongly upon *your* life?

In the crises of life, it's easy to tell who has the Word abiding in them and who doesn't. And those who speak the Word without any anointing upon it are usually the ones who just give mental assent to the Word. They mentally agree with everything the Word says, but they have not taken the time to really put God's Word in their hearts. So when they speak, no power is released. The Word doesn't have the anointing on it that it should.

I want to show you the power of the anointed Word of God. I will never forget the evening my family stood around my grandmother's bed as she lay dying. My dad had prayed to the Lord some years before and said, "Lord, she's never had anything in life, and now I'm just getting to the place where I can do something for her, and she's about ready to come home to be with You. I don't want her to go yet. Please let her live to be 80 years old, so I can try to make up to her for some of the things she's had to go through in life."

The Lord answered that prayer. My grandmother turned 80 in September 1972, and she went to be with the Lord that October. You could see her health begin to fail as soon as she turned 80 years old. It was just as if someone had turned off the well of life.

The night my grandmother passed away, the family stood around her hospital bed. We all watched as she drew her last breath, and then she was gone to be with the Lord. The whole family began to cry in grief at her passing. But just then I began to hear a rumbling as though someone were speaking, just very slowly, very quietly at first. And then it began to get louder. I realized that my dad was quoting the Word of God. The scriptures began to flow out of him: *"O death, where is thy sting? O grave, where is thy victory?" "Precious in the sight of the Lord is the death of his saints"* (1 Cor. 15:55; Ps. 116:15). On and on he quoted God's Word.

Of course the family was sad — we were all going to miss my grandmother. But as those words came forth, the sweet Presence of the Holy Spirit came into that room and calmed everyone's grief. Even the nurses commented, "There is a different atmosphere in this room than we've ever experienced when someone has just died."

What made the difference? God's irresistible, anointed Word! God's Word has power to bring comfort and help in times of stress and difficulty. The right and privilege to speak God's Word with power to effect change to God's glory — whatever the situation might be — belongs to every member of the Body of Christ. If you are born again, that privilege belongs to you!

Many times when the enemy tries to come in like a flood upon our lives in times of crises or in the tests and trials of life, our tendency is to get into the natural. But if we'll keep our minds renewed, we'll be able to stay in the Spirit during those difficult times.

However, don't feel guilty and let the devil try to condemn you if you get over into the natural for a moment during a time of crisis. All of us have experienced that at one time or another. But the secret of success is not remaining in the natural! Immediately realize that you're thinking, talking, and reacting out of the natural man, and get right back into the Spirit because that's where the victories are *won* and *maintained.*

Speaking God's Word will bring you into a new arena in life. If you will meditate on God's Word and take the time to hide it in your heart, you will find that things which used to cause you problems in life, will begin to fade away. God's Word has power and authority! It cannot be resisted! Your life can be filled with joy and happiness. You can receive from God exactly what He has promised to you in His Word. All the promises of God already belong to you through your inheritance in Christ.

Another secret to being able to speak the irresistible Word of God with power is to be full of the love of God. In America we use the word "love" so casually. We say, "I *love* candy," or "I *love* my car," or "I *love* my wife." But I'm talking about a lifestyle of practicing the love of God on a daily basis, and sometimes that requires sacrificial giving or loving, even when it hurts. "... *God so loved the world, that he GAVE* ..." (John 3:16). Also, God so loved that He *for*gave.

When we allow the love of God to begin to operate in our lives, we will be able to freely forgive others too. It's not always easy to forgive; sometimes it's difficult. Sometimes loving someone when there's no apparent change in the circumstances will test your love walk! But as we practice God's love, we learn to forgive those who have done us wrong — or maybe are *still* doing us wrong. We will not be able to speak God's irresistible Word or receive from God if we don't have love in our hearts.

If you walk in love, you will not be able to harbor grudges against those who may have wronged you. "Well, I'll tell you one thing! I may forgive him, but I'll never *forget* what he did to me!" That's not love! Yes, the things people do and say sometimes hurt us. Stinging, malicious words can even cause an inner wound. But if we learn how to let the love of God flow out to others in forgiveness, we can pray for those who have wronged us. You will never speak irresistible words without learning to walk in love.

It needs to become a colossal truth to you, one that you incorporate into your life daily, that *you* can speak God's irresistible Word of power and anointing. *You* can speak God's irresistible Word of power, and nothing on earth can resist God's Word! But, remember, God doesn't give you the ability to speak His Word with authority and power just so you can make a name for yourself or so that you can exalt yourself. If that's your motive, watch out! No, God gives you the authority to speak His Word with power so you can experience for yourself that God's Word works, and then you can go out and set other people free.

With God's Word, you can change things in your life! You don't have to live a life of lack, always beaten down by the devil and oppressed by your circumstances. When you speak God's Word, there is nothing on earth that can resist the Word or stand against it! The Word of God will make you an effective witness. The irresistible Word of God will meet your financial needs. The Word of God will heal you, and bring deliverance, health, and peace of mind, because "by His stripes you are healed" (Isa. 53:5).

What is it that *you* have needed from God? Dare to put His Word to work in your situation!

Perhaps Satan has had a heyday in your life, and you feel as if he's almost run you down with his wicked maneuvers and schemes. Perhaps you feel that he's walked all over you for so long that what's the use? If the devil's been running over your life for a long time, you're going to have to show him you mean business!

I want to remind you that the enemy is already a defeated foe. Jesus conquered him at the Cross, and through Jesus Christ *you* have authority over him *now*. You just need to begin to speak God's Word and put him in his place! The first time you speak, you may not see any visible change in your circumstances. You may have to steadfastly speak God's Word over your situation because if the devil has been having a heyday in your life for a long time, he's not going to want to leave overnight. He's going to see if *you* believe what you say! But as you continue to put God's irresistible Word down on the inside of you in your heart, you will be able to rise up and speak words that will demolish all of the enemy's plans and schemes in your life!

Do not get discouraged! You are going to have to use your authority — the authority that Jesus Christ bought and paid for — against the devil!

God taught me something about exercising the authority which we already possess, in a very practical way. At one time we had a cocker spaniel named Penny. When Penny did something wrong, I could say halfheartedly to her all day long, "Penny, please don't do that," and she would just sit there and ignore me. She wouldn't pay the slightest bit of attention to me. We went through a time with Penny when we realized that we were not taking our proper authority with her, and that's why she wasn't paying any attention to us when we gave her a command. So we began to put some force and authority behind our words when we commanded her.

Instead of just saying, "Penny, no," we began to say, "NO, PENNY! DON'T DO THAT!!!" By the tone and the authority of our voices, she knew she'd better obey!

Exercising your authority works that way with the devil too. If you rebuke him halfheartedly with no authority or power behind your words, he's not going to take you seriously. But when the Word of God has become real in your life, and *you know who you are in Christ* and the Word has become a vital, living truth on the inside of you, then you will speak the Word of God with the anointing of God! *Then* watch the devil back down! He knows he is a defeated foe, but much of the time God's people act like *they* don't know it!

God's Word says that by His stripes we were healed (Isa. 53:5). God's Word says that by the shed blood of Jesus on Calvary some 2,000 years ago, mankind can be saved, healed, and delivered. God said that He sent His Word and He healed us (Ps. 107:20). The anointing and the Word of God bring deliverance. God also promises us that our needs can be met. *The Amplified Bible* says that God will liberally supply or *fill to the full* our every need (Phil. 4:19). But people must accept the Word of God and believe it in order for it to work for them. You see, salvation and healing are available, but people must believe it in order to enjoy the benefits already provided for them!

You must believe that the irresistible Word of God is there for your benefit to help you and to bless your life.

Jesus said He came to bring us abundant life — peace, joy, love, and well-being (John 10:10). Jesus Christ is the same yesterday, today, and forever — for *you* (Heb. 13:8). If you believe that, you can receive from God, and God's Word will work for you.

However, again I must emphasize that God's Word always works in line with His nature and His character, so you won't be able to speak irresistible words — words that change things — without God's love operating in your life. But as your lifestyle lines up with the Word of God, and as you daily practice walking in love, you will see the irresistible power of God's Word manifesting abundant life in every area and in every circumstance of your life.

I believe that when the Body of Christ begins to speak God's Word with the anointing and with the authority that Christ has given us, we will begin to witness the greatest revival this world has ever known. And as people are born again into the Kingdom of God, God's Word will generate such a holy fervor and have such a tremendous effect upon the earth, that in the thrones of glory the heavenly Father will lean over to Jesus and say, "Son, it's time for You to go get Your Bride!"

I believe as the Body of Christ begins to speak the irresistible Word of God, and as we march forward fulfilling the goals and purposes God has for each one of our lives, one day we'll look up into the eastern sky and we're going to hear a resounding shout from our Savior! And we're all going home to be with Him forever!

Irresistible words! Jesus' shout will be of such a quality and such a magnitude that it will wake up those in the grave, and the Bible says they will be caught up first and then we which are alive and remain shall be caught up together with Him in the clouds of glory. So shall we ever be with the Lord (1 Thess. 4:16,17).

Do you want to be ready for Jesus' return? Begin to speak the irresistible Word of God with power to set men and women free! Begin to consecrate yourself as never before to do God's will on the earth. Let's get ourselves ready for the Bridegroom who is coming for a Bride without spot or wrinkle (Eph. 5:27).

I believe the Body of Christ is on the verge of one of the greatest revivals that has ever shaken this earth, and it will come about because Christians have taken the time to set themselves aside in prayer and Bible study, to consecrate themselves in holiness unto God, and to speak God's irresistible Word with power and authority!

Begin to meditate on God's Word and put it down deep in your heart and begin to speak His Word over your life. God's Word is full of power; it's full of grace; and it's full of life! God's Word is anointed to carry out God's plan for *your* life. God's Word is anointed to fulfill and to bring to pass everything *you* need it to accomplish in *your* life.

Speak God's Word over those situations which have so perplexed you and defeated you in life. As you are diligent to hide the Word in your heart and to speak it with your mouth, and as you move more and more into a lifestyle that is consistent with God's nature, watch God's Word unravel and demolish the problems in your life in its unspeakable, irresistible fashion. God's Word is irrefutable and it will not return void in your life. Put God's Word to work! It will not fail you!

The *Word of Faith* is a full-color magazine
with faith-building teaching articles by
Rev. Kenneth E. Hagin and Rev. Kenneth Hagin Jr.

The *Word of Faith* also includes encouraging true-life
stories of Christians overcoming circumstances
through God's Word, and information on the
various outreaches of Kenneth Hagin Ministries
and RHEMA Bible Church.

To receive a free subscription to *The Word of Faith*, call:
1-888-28-FAITH — Offer #864
(1-888-283-2484)
www.rhema.org

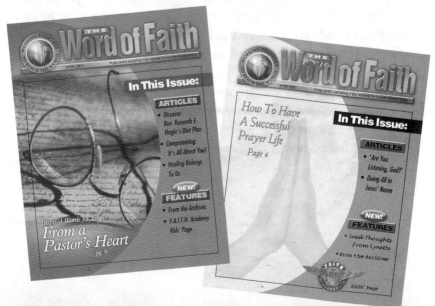